# Pupil Book 5
# Vocabulary, Grammar and Punctuation

Author: Abigail Steel

William Collins' dream of knowledge for all began with the publication of his first book in 1819. A self-educated mill worker, he not only enriched millions of lives, but also founded a flourishing publishing house. Today, staying true to this spirit, Collins books are packed with inspiration, innovation and practical expertise. They place you at the centre of a world of possibility and give you exactly what you need to explore it.

Collins. Freedom to teach.

Published by Collins
An imprint of HarperCollins*Publishers*
The News Building
1 London Bridge Street
London
SE1 9GF

Browse the complete Collins catalogue at
**www.collins.co.uk**

ISBN 978-0-00-813332-0

British Library Cataloguing in Publication Data
A Catalogue record for this publication is available from the British Library

Edited by Hannah Hirst-Dunton
Cover design and artwork by Amparo Barrera
Internal design concept by Amparo Barrera
Typesetting by Jouve India Private Ltd
Illustrations by Beatriz Castro, Aptara and QBS

Printed in Italy by Grafica Veneta S.p.A.

# Contents

# Expanded noun phrases

We use **expanded noun phrases** to give more information about nouns. A noun can be expanded using adjectives before it and extra information (a preposition phrase) after it.

- Noun: dog

- Noun phrase: the dog

- With adjectives: the **hairy**, **brown** dog

- With a preposition phrase: the hairy, brown dog **with muddy paws**

## Get started

Copy and expand these noun phrases, adding two suitable adjectives before the nouns. One has been done for you.

1. the _green, scaly_ snake

2. a _____ storm

3. my _____ mattress

4. the _____ apple

5. a _____ child

6. that _____table

7. Sorrell's _____ coat

8. our _____ poodle

9. Liam's _____ bag

10. one _____ morning

## Try these

Copy out these sentences and expand the underlined noun phrases, adding preposition phrases after the nouns. One has been done for you.

1. It was while we were hiking by a lake that we saw <u>the green, scaly snake</u> *with the flickering tongue.*

2. Rather than buy something new for the party, Keesha wanted to wear <u>her favourite old dress</u> . . .

3. Rashan was horrified – completely by accident, he had broken <u>his dad's shiny new watch</u> . . .

4. There is no easy way of finding out exactly what is hidden in <u>our messy garden shed</u> . . .

5. Looking up, we saw a robin building a nest in <u>that tall, leafy tree</u> . . .

6. Even though she was in the next room, Jo couldn't help but hear <u>Natalya's loud, high-pitched giggle</u> . . .

7. Feeling a little bit nervous, Jean-Pierre walked into the classroom of <u>his new primary school</u> . . .

8. George stood on tiptoes, reached on top of the bookcase and carefully took down <u>the dusty, tattered book</u> . . .

## Now try these

Expand each noun with adjectives and a preposition phrase, and then use it in a sentence.

1. cave
2. treehouse
3. motorbike
4. library
5. pony
6. costume
7. story

# Changing nouns or adjectives into verbs

Some **nouns** and **adjectives** can be turned into **verbs** using **suffixes**. A suffix is a letter or group of letters that goes at the end of a word to make a new word. Sometimes the suffix is added without the root word changing, but sometimes the root word has to be changed too.

- strength     + en       = strengthen
  (noun        + suffix    = verb)

The root word is most commonly changed by deleting the letter y at the end of a word.

- accesso**ry**    + ise       = accessorise
  (adjective     + suffix     = verb)

## Get started

Look at each of the verbs on the left. Match each verb to the root word from which it is made. One has been done for you.

| | | |
|---|---|---|
| **1.** *communicate* | **a)** pure | |
| **2.** purify | **b)** strength | |
| **3.** horrify | **c)** ripe | |
| **4.** ripen | **d)** *communication* | |
| **5.** categorise | **e)** drama | |
| **6.** strengthen | **f)** medicine | |
| **7.** dramatise | **g)** category | |
| **8.** medicate | **h)** horror | |

## Try these

Copy and complete these sentences by changing the word in brackets into the correct verb, using a suffix from the box. One has been done for you.

| -ate | -en | -ise | -ify |
|------|-----|------|------|

1. The shops will _advertise_ the January sale shortly. (advert)

2. The strawberry mousse will _____ in the fridge. (solid)

3. We have been working very hard to understand when we should and should not _____ words with prefixes. (hyphen)

4. My dad loves to play tricks and _____ me! (fright)

5. Our teacher wanted to _____ the way we presented our homework. (standard)

6. Cleaning your teeth every day will help keep them healthy and also _____ them. (bright)

7. The children needed to _____ their project work under different topic headings. (class)

8. The whole school was working to _____ the hall for the summer concert. (decor)

9. Can we confirm and _____ our plans concerning getting to the bus stop for the school trip? (final)

10. The soldiers worked hard throughout the night to _____ the king's castle. (fort)

## Now try these

Change each word into a verb and then use it in a sentence.

1. magnification
2. apology
3. less
4. active
5. animation
6. flat
7. simple
8. minimum

# Verb prefixes

A **prefix** is a group of letters that can be added to the beginning of a word to change its meaning.

- **mis**behave = behave badly (**mis-** means 'badly' or 'incorrectly')

- **re**appear = appear again (**re-** means 'again' or 'back')

## Get started

Look at each word's prefix. Write a definition for the word and then put it into a sentence. One has been done for you.

1. rebuild

   Answer: *To rebuild means to build again. I will rebuild my sandcastle.*

2. rewrite

3. replace

4. reopen

5. repay

6. misdirect

7. misestimate

8. misadvise

9. misjudge

10. misuse

## Try these

Copy and complete these sentences, adding a prefix from the box below to the word in brackets. One has been done for you.

> de-    re-    mis-    dis-    over-

1. My friend Suki and her brother Jay <u>disagreed</u> quite seriously yesterday morning. (agreed)

2. Leon had come to play rehearsals without his script, which really _____ our director. (pleased)

3. We had to hold sports day when the weather was boiling, so we drank lots of water to make sure we didn't _____ in the heat. (hydrate)

4. I really am trying hard not to _____ to what you just said, but I'm so cross! (react)

5. Your dinner has gone cold now, but I can _____ it for you in a few minutes. (heat)

6. Lucas was asked to _____ some homework he had done badly. (write)

7. It was very difficult walking through town today – the sales are really _____ the streets. (crowding)

8. Mr Melchett _____ the study because he'd left his glasses in there. (entered)

## Now try these

Add the same prefix (**de-**, **re-**, **over-**, **dis-** or **mis-**) to all the words in each word bank and then use them all in a short paragraph.

1. trust, honour, approve

2. inform, place, understand

3. direct, apply, activate

4. fill, eat, cook

5. bone, frost, code

# Formal and informal language

We use **formal language** to speak to people that we don't know and to write letters. We use **informal language** to talk to friends and to write emails and texts.

- **Informal**: contractions, incomplete sentences, words missed out, shorter words and slang

- **Formal**: no contractions, only complete sentences, careful word choices, polite and respectful language

## Get started

Copy out each sentence. Then label it 'formal' or 'informal'. One has been done for you.

1. D'ya fancy watchin' that alien film? *informal*

2. I have told you, please do not talk when you are working in the library.

3. I've said, no talking in t' library!

4. I would like to request a meeting at your earliest convenience.

5. The performance will resume at 8pm promptly.

6. You OK?

7. What you up to Tuesday coming?

8. Do you think you will be able to attend?

## Try these

Copy out the more informal sentence from each pair. One has been done for you.

1. **a)** Watchin' that rocket launch on TV tonight?

    **b)** Are you planning to watch that rocket launch on the television tonight?

    Answer: *Watchin' that rocket launch on TV tonight?*

2. **a)** Do not worry about what she has said in the past.

    **b)** Don't worry 'bout what she said.

3. **a)** Lots to tell yer!

    **b)** I have lots to tell you.

4. **a)** Please let me know as soon as possible.

    **b)** Let me know ASAP.

5. **a)** What did you say?

    **b)** What?

6. **a)** D'ya have your mobile?

    **b)** Do you have your mobile phone with you?

## Now try these

Rewrite each sentence in a formal style by changing the underlined words.

1. What <u>d'ya</u> think <u>'bout</u> that new film?

2. Did you say <u>you'd</u> seen something good on <u>TV</u>?

3. <u>I'm</u> not <u>doin'</u> anything wrong.

4. <u>They're</u> saying <u>you'd</u> seen it.

5. Is it <u>OK</u> for our plans that <u>it's s'posed</u> to be raining on Saturday?

6. I know <u>you're</u> just joking, but <u>you'd</u> better calm down <u>ASAP</u>!

# Adverbs and modal verbs showing possibility

Adverbs and modal verbs can show how likely the action of a verb is.

- **Adverbs**: perhaps, maybe, possibly, probably, definitely, certainly, surely

- **Modal verbs**: can, could, may, might, shall, should, will, would

## Get started

Copy out these sentences, underlining the modal verbs and adverbs. One has been done for you.

1. "<u>Surely</u> there's something fun we can do this weekend," I said to Dad.

2. Dad looked at the weather forecast and finally made a suggestion: we could go sailing!

3. "I might agree," Mum replied with a smile.

4. I certainly wanted to go – I've loved our sailing holidays ever since I was a little girl.

5. Dad said he could probably borrow his friend's sailing boat.

6. "Shall we invite Grandpa, too?" I asked Dad.

7. He replied that we definitely should.

8. "Grandpa would probably be a great help," he added.

## Try these

Copy out the sentence from each pair that seems most likely. One has been done for you.

1. **a)** Perhaps I'll go home.

   **b)** I'll probably go home.

    Answer: *I'll probably go home.*

2. **a)** We will follow her.

   **b)** We might follow her.

3. **a)** I could help.

   **b)** I should help.

4. **a)** Maybe you'll win!

   **b)** You'll definitely win!

5. **a)** I can come with you into town.

   **b)** I may come with you into town.

6. **a)** I shall go to the shops with Gran and help her carry her bags.

   **b)** I would go to the shops with Gran and help her carry her bags.

## Now try these

Answer each question with two sentences, one using a modal verb and one using an adverb, to show how likely the actions of your verbs are.

1. Will the weather be nice at the weekend?

2. Are you going on holiday this year?

3. What are you doing tomorrow evening?

4. After school, will you go straight home?

5. Would you like to learn to scuba dive?

6. What do you think you'll do for your birthday?

# Relative clauses

We use **relative clauses** to give more information about nouns. We can start a relative clause with a **relative pronoun** (who, that, which, whose) or a **relative adverb** (where, when). Sometimes there will be a comma in front of a relative clause, but not always.

- There's my neighbour, **who** won the sprint race at school.

- Look at my house, **which** has a red door and a brass letterbox.

## Get started

Copy out these sentences and underline the relative pronoun or relative adverb. One has been done for you.

1. Priya is my neighbour, <u>who</u> comes with me to football training.

2. Today is our annual school sports day, which is always exciting.

3. Faye is an amazing athlete, whose trainers are always falling apart.

4. Band practice starts at six o'clock, when my favourite programme is over – luckily!

5. Today is the day when I start my new reading programme.

6. I will be walking over the mountains, where the explorers walked!

7. This is the album that I want to buy with my pocket money.

8. My cousin is the girl whose jumper is covered in bright red polka dots.

## Try these

Copy out these sentences, underlining the relative clause in each. One has been done for you.

1. Devon is a seaside county <u>where people often go on holiday</u>.

2. These are the trainers that I bought.

3. Pratik, who lives with his mum, has been helping.

4. Look at these photos that I took of Millie.

5. I have a friend who is an amazing singer.

6. Salma handed her glasses, which were broken, to her PE teacher.

7. Damara's art partner was Marek, whose paintings were always the best.

8. It was almost 8.30 a.m., when the alarm would go off.

## Now try these

Copy and complete these sentences by finishing the relative clause.

1. Mr Prabhakar is the running coach who . . .

2. We were in the aisle of the supermarket where . . .

3. I would like to buy some new trainers that . . .

4. My fiercest competition is a girl who . . .

5. This month is also the month when . . .

6. In the crowd was my step-dad, whose . . .

# Linking words in a paragraph

**Paragraphs** make a long piece of writing easier to read. A paragraph is a group of sentences about one idea or topic.

We often use special words to help the reader understand the **connections** between ideas in a piece of writing. We can use **linking words and phrases** to help the reader see these connections between sentences and clauses in a paragraph.

- Phrases:
  - **First of all** . . .
  - **After that** . . .
  - **Finally** . . .

- Linking words:
  - . . . **so** . . .
  - . . . **but** . . .
  - . . . **because** . . .

## Get started

These sentences link together to form a paragraph. Copy out the sentences and underline the linking words and phrases. One has been done for you.

1. *In the beginning*, the swimming pool was open every day.

2. It was popular, but it needed money for repairs.

3. After that, it could not afford to open more than three days a week.

4. Now, unless we raise more money, the swimming pool will be demolished.

5. We will, as a result, not have anywhere to go swimming.

6. Next, we will try a new plan: we will hold a charity street party.

7. Finally, people have noticed our efforts and they have bought hundreds of tickets.

8. Because of this, the council has offered to double our money.

## Try these

Copy and complete these sentences by adding connecting adverbials or conjunctions to create a paragraph about a day out. One has been done for you.

1. *First of all,* we went on the swings *and then* on the seesaw.

2. We had a great time _____.

3. We stopped _____ I wanted a drink.

4. We stopped for lunch_____.

5. _____ we walked around the forest.

6. _____ it was cold.

7. We got back to the bus stop _____.

8. _____, we went home _____ I was shattered.

## Now try these

Use linking words and phrases to write the following:

1. One short paragraph about a new species of insect.

2. One short paragraph about a new theme-park ride.

3. One short paragraph about a club or sport you enjoy.

4. One short paragraph about making some food.

5. One short paragraph about what you have done today.

6. One short paragraph about what you plan to do next week.

# Adverbials

**Adverbials** of time, place, manner or number can show when, how long, where, how and in which order things happen. They can be single words (adverbs) or adverbial phrases.

- **Every day**, Jack and Jill **rapidly** walked **up the hill**.

- **Firstly**, they sat **under a tree**.

## Get started

Copy out these sentences, underlining the adverbials. One has been done for you.

1. <u>Last month</u>, Katka's family moved house.

2. They moved to a large stone farmhouse in the countryside.

3. After the move, they discovered some nasty problems.

4. Unfortunately, the water pipes were very old.

5. They are still working, however.

6. Katka's dad has found a leak only once.

7. Gradually, they will get the pipes fixed.

8. Katka really loves living at the farm.

## Try these

Copy and expand these sentences by adding adverbials that give the details stated. One has been done for you.

1. Add an adverbial phrase that shows **place** to this sentence:

   Katka keeps chickens.

   Answer: *Katka keeps chickens in the garden.*

2. Add an adverbial phrase that shows **time** to this sentence:

   Visitors can come to stay.

3. Add an adverbial phrase that shows **manner** to this sentence:

   The house has lots of rooms.

4. Add another adverbial phrase that shows **place** to this sentence:

   The children can run wild.

5. Add another adverbial phrase that shows **time** to this sentence:

   There are lots of tasks to do.

6. Add another adverbial phrase that shows **manner** to this sentence:

   The whole family enjoys helping out.

## Now try these

Copy and expand these sentences, putting one adverbial of time and one adverbial of place in each.

1. Emma redecorated her house.
2. There was lots of junk to clear out.
3. She worked hard to paint the walls.
4. Emma chose a rug and new curtains.
5. The family was pleased with the result.
6. Emma's mum held a house-warming party.

# Using commas for clearer meaning

**Commas** can be useful to make the meaning of sentences clearer. They show small breaks between words, phrases or clauses. We also use them to separate items in lists.

- After we ate, my brother was full.
- I had chocolate, a biscuit and an apple.

## Get started

Copy and complete these sentences by adding commas. One has been done for you.

1. *I would like to visit Norway, Poland and Latvia.*

2. To bake a cake you need eggs flour and sugar.

3. To be safe on a climbing trip you should take a friend ropes and water.

4. Some of the chores you could do include tidying vacuuming and polishing.

5. An ancient pirate treasure chest could contain gold silver and emeralds.

6. At school today we learned lots of new skills in Maths English and Science.

7. My favourite sports clubs to attend after school are tennis zumba and athletics.

8. Before I can go to bed I have to practise my drumming spelling and times tables.

## Try these

Copy and complete these sentences by adding a comma after the adverbial. One has been done for you.

1. *When I am older, I would like to travel all around the world.*

2. Every Thursday I bake a cake to take to my book club.

3. If the weather gets better I might go climbing this weekend.

4. When I need some extra money I do more chores around the house.

5. Even though I've spent a long time looking I've never found any of the treasure.

6. With a sudden rush my cousin bolted into the room.

7. Under the sofa we found the model car I had lost last year.

8. Twice a day I make sure I brush my teeth.

## Now try these

Copy and complete these sentences by adding commas around the relative clauses. One has been done for you.

1. The pirate, whose loot we were hunting, was catching up with us.

2. It all started when some diamonds which were incredibly valuable had gone missing.

3. In a moment when I hadn't even been concentrating I'd worked out where they must be.

4. My quest which was very risky was to track them.

5. The sea-captain with me who was new to the job was nervous.

6. Lost Island where the jewels were buried seemed deserted.

# Hyphens

**Compound words** are words made from two or more shorter words. They have one unit of meaning. Compound **nouns** do not usually have a **hyphen** (-).

- A **football** is a ball you kick with your **foot**.

We do use hyphens to join words that make compound **adjectives**.

- The **man-eating** crocodile lurked on the bank of the deep river.

- The **rosy-cheeked** children sang and danced in the park.

## Get started

Copy out these sentences, underlining the compound word in each one. These compound words do not have hyphens. One has been done for you.

1. *This morning, our <u>headteacher</u> said he had an exciting new scheme to challenge us.*

2. He said the school had won some money, and asked us to design a new school playground.

3. For the last two years, I have been the goalkeeper in our school team.

4. Therefore, of course, I designed a large grassy area to act as a huge football pitch.

5. The day they revealed the winner, we had a great party outdoors with music and cakes.

6. The newspaper reporter came to report on the event.

7. She wanted to conduct an interview with the prizewinner.

8. The winning design – which was not mine – included a big classroom space in the fresh air.

## Try these

Look at each pair of phrases. Copy out the phrases that use hyphens correctly. One has been done for you.

1. **a)** The short-sighted man

   **b)** The short sighted man

   Answer: *The short-sighted man*

2. **a)** Our city centre school

   **b)** Our city-centre school

3. **a)** Pretty gold hair

   **b)** Pretty-gold hair

4. **a)** The kind-hearted girl

   **b)** The kind hearted girl

5. **a)** The kind old man

   **b)** The kind-old man

6. **a)** One two-year-old child

   **b)** One two year-old child

7. **a)** The dish washing sponge

   **b)** The dish-washing sponge

8. **a)** A happy go-lucky smile

   **b)** A happy-go-lucky smile

## Now try these

Change each phrase into a description that uses a hyphenated compound adjective. Then use it in a sentence.

1. Paint that dries quickly
2. Cow that has brown spots
3. Mouse with three legs
4. Man who eats fire
5. Bird with yellow feathers
6. Lizard with a long neck

# Brackets, dashes and commas

Brackets (( )), dashes (–) and commas (,) can all be used in a sentence to separate a word, phrase or clause that gives extra detail. This is called **parenthesis**.

- The party (held in a posh hotel) was great.

- The party – held in a posh hotel – was great.

- The party, held in a posh hotel, was great.

## Get started

Copy out these sentences, underlining the parenthesis. One has been done for you.

1. *A photograph (which showed the position of hidden treasure) was discovered under the floorboards.*

2. The boy – Dominic – made a clever and daring plan.

3. He stowed away, before anyone could see him, on a ship.

4. The captain (who was very clever, too) discovered him.

5. Dominic told the captain – who was utterly fascinated – about the photograph.

6. Together, and with the rest of the ship's crew, they decided to set out in search of the treasure.

7. They had a long, hard journey (which was to be expected), but they bore up well.

8. Finally – just when they were giving up hope – they saw land.

## Try these

Copy out these sentences, adding punctuation around the underlined examples of parenthesis. One has been done for you.

1. *The sea, <u>with its cruel nature</u>, had been unforgiving.*

2. The island <u>which they had been seeking</u> was in the distance.

3. The ship disappeared <u>all of a sudden</u> into some thick fog.

4. The captain who was <u>looking around in confusion</u> was worried.

5. His crew <u>who had been right next to him</u> were now nowhere to be seen.

6. Then <u>with a great start</u> he heard his first mate's voice.

7. The first mate <u>a tall, strong man</u> was still close by.

8. When the fog cleared <u>finally blown away to sea</u> everyone could see what had happened.

## Now try these

Copy out these sentences, adding some extra information in parenthesis.

1. Our basketball game was ruined by a storm.

2. I am planning a birthday party.

3. The new girl is sitting at my project table.

4. I was starving when I got home.

5. Maya would try to have an early night.

6. The science exam will be held on Thursday morning.

# Boundaries between clauses

We can use a **colon (:)**, **semi-colon (;)** or **dash (–)** to separate main clauses, instead of full stops or conjunctions.

**Semi-colons (;)** show linked clauses that are equally important. For example:

> The school bus is usually late; it was late again today.

**Colons (:)** introduce reasons or examples. For example:

> The school bus was late today: it had a flat tyre.

**Dashes (–)** can be used instead, in informal writing. For example:

> The school bus was late – now we'll be late for school!

## Get started

Copy out the example from each pair that is an independent clause. One has been done for you.

1. **a)** There was a pram standing in the hall

   **b)** Because there was a pram standing in the hall

   Answer: *There was a pram standing in the hall*

2. **a)** Great!

   **b)** That is great!

3. **a)** Once my aunt and my little sister are finally back at home

   **b)** My aunt and my little sister are finally back at home

4. **a)** Singing her song very loudly

   **b)** Sue-Ann was singing her song very loudly

5. **a)** Louis arrived with his friend from Scouts

   **b)** With his friend from Scouts

6. **a)** The desert island was beautiful

   **b)** A beautiful desert island

## Try these

Copy and complete these sentences by adding a colon, semi-colon or dash between the two independent clauses. One has been done for you.

1. *Mum had an idea: we could play a game.*

2. Pavel grinned he liked games.

3. He chose a red counter I chose a green one.

4. Pavel was doing well he kept rolling high numbers.

5. Then I caught up I won!

6. We may play again I'll be more confident next time.

7. Perhaps Dad would like to play as well he likes games too.

8. We should play outside now though the weather has not cleared up.

## Now try these

Copy and complete these sentences by adding a suitable independent clause.

1. They carried on:

2. The wind blew hard –

3. The dog ran on ahead;

4. A deer appeared beside them:

5. They thought they would be OK –

6. They finally got back to the town;

# Colons to introduce lists

A **colon (:)** can be used in different ways. We can use a colon to introduce a list.

- I like three sports: football, snooker and cricket.

- Dan collected things: coloured marbles, rocks and paperclips.

## Get started

Copy and complete these lists by adding the correct punctuation. One has been done for you.

1. I bought some new stationery for my return to school in September: fountain pens, pencils of different strengths, a shatterproof ruler and an eraser shaped like a snail.

2. Gran got some tasty-looking fruit at the market today some red apples some juicy pears some bananas some oranges and lots of green grapes

3. Freya happily packed her little suitcase in preparation for her family holiday that summer a bright swimsuit a towel cool sunglasses and her high-strength sun cream

4. I have lots of things to read on the long train journey to my cousin's house books comics a magazine and my tablet

5. We bought lots of things for our lazy Sunday breakfast orange juice with bits grapefruits fresh croissants and natural yoghurt

6. The weather was really horrid last week icily cold very windy really foggy and wet everywhere

### Try these

Copy and complete these sentences, adding punctuation and a suitable list after the introduction. One has been done for you.

1. Types of shoes I own: *trainers, sandals, pumps and boots.*

2. My absolute favourite foods are

3. I took some of my favourite books with me

4. These are my favourite films of all time

5. My favourite apps on my phone at the moment are

6. I bought several small presents for my grandfather's birthday

7. The bouquet Tracey had been sent contained lots of flowers

8. We heard four different instruments on the CD

## Now try these

For each topic, write a sentence that includes an introduction followed by a list. Use the correct punctuation.

1. A tasty recipe

2. Rides at a theme park

3. Chores to do

4. Games to play

5. Fun sports

6. Songs you know

# Punctuating bulleted lists

We can use **bullet points** to organise a list so that it is clear to read and understand. There are three main rules:

- If the list starts with an introduction, put a colon after it.

- Each list item starts with a bullet point.

- Each item is written on a new line, one below the other.

## Get started

Copy out each sentence about bullet-pointed lists. Then label it 'true' or 'false', to show whether it is correct. One has been done for you.

1. Items must be in full sentences. *false*

2. Bullet-pointed lists can be clearer to read.

3. Each item must end in a comma.

4. Items are written below each other.

5. A bullet point starts each item.

6. If the list starts with an introduction, you should end the introduction with a colon.

7. You should never use any punctuation in list items.

8. You should never use a bullet in front of the last item in your list.

## Try these

Rewrite these lists as correctly punctuated, bullet-pointed lists. One has been done for you.

1. These are my things to do: make my bed, hang up my coat, clean my shoes.

   Answer: *These are my things to do:*

   - *make my bed*

   - *hang up my coat*

   - *clean my shoes*

2. Things I need new: a ruler, white socks, hair bobbles

3. I have lots of exercises planned: ten star-jumps, a ten-minute jog, a long bike ride

4. Seeds I need to sow in my little patch of the garden: carrots, lettuces, tomato

5. Some British coins: £2, 50p, 20p, 10p, 2p

6. My close relatives are: my dad, my step-mum, my sister, my step-brother, my half-brother

7. There are lots of foods I enjoy: sweetcorn, mashed potato, peanut butter, oranges, Turkish delight

8. My gym kit: a swimsuit for swimming, a leotard for gymnastics, shorts and polo shirt for netball, indoor and outdoor trainers

## Now try these

Copy out each introduction and add a bullet-pointed list after it.

1. I would like to visit these countries when I am older:

2. There are lots of games you could play:

3. Lots of different animals live in the jungle:

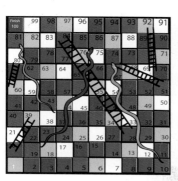